SZENTENDRE

SZENTENDRE

With 101 colour photographs by Gyula Tahin
and an introduction by Stojan Vujičić

Corvina Kiadó

3rd edition

Original title: Szentendre
Corvina Kiadó, Budapest, 1985
Translated by Zsuzsa Béres
Translation revised by J. E. Sollosy
Design by Erzsébet Szabados

ISBN 963 13 2426 5

Dawn on the church spires glitters,
Ruffled houses in purple light do glow,
The Danube's waves lap slowly by the shore...

(István Vas: Szentendre Elegy)

We of Szentendre, renowned throughout the world!

(from an 18th-century Serb folk song)

"Do you know where Szentendre is?" This was how Jakov Ignjatović (1822–1889), a native of Szentendre, began one of his most popular novels over a hundred years ago. He then continued: "This small town is situated on the right bank of the Danube, between Buda, Visegrád and Esztergom. A magnificent landscape! In front of the town is the Little Danube, that is, a branch of the Danube. Before our eyes stretches an island dappled with fertile villages. Beyond this the Big Danube lies. And to the left and beyond the small town the enchanting spectacle of vineyards and splendid hills that face the forests of Visegrád. And then that lovely valley between Szentendre, Pomáz and Buda, reminiscent of a huge amphitheatre, with ancient white Budavár rising nearby. Then Pest, facing Buda. Delightful landscape, prosperity, superb wines, heavenly water. Who could ask for anything more?"

Situated at a convenient distance from Budapest, Szentendre nestles among the eastern slopes of the Pilis Mountain Range. Occupying a semicircular area sealed off by the Danube, the location of this enchanting small town indeed reminds one of an amphitheatre created by nature.

Szentendre is the gateway to the captivating and picturesque Danube Bend—in fact the road to the region's historical towns, Visegrád and Esztergom, passes through Szentendre. The closed formation of the historical town core, which was built on the hillside, creates a castle-like impression on the steep bank of the Szentendre branch of the Danube. On the other hand, the labyrinth of irregularly shaped whimsically meandering cobble-stone streets, narrow alleys, winding ascents and steep stairways impart a distinctly Mediterranean character to the town, evoking the atmosphere of Dalmatian, Greek and Italian coastal towns.

The neighbourhood of the town situated on the bank of the Danube also reveals this duality. To the north-west a mountainous region, reaching six hundred metres in height, accentuates the landscape, which descends towards the river bank in gentle, terraced slopes. Facing the river bank and stretching as far as Visegrád lies Szentendre Island. To the west rise the fascinating volcanic rock columns of Kőhegy.

The town is divided by the Bükkös Stream, while further to the north the Stara Voda Stream rushes into the Danube beyond Pap Island.

Szentendre and its vicinity has been a populated area since ancient times. The fact that there had been important settlements around this area in the course of four thousand years, between the Neolithic Age and the Roman era, is supported by a wealth of archaeological evidence. The Illyrians appeared in the 1st millennium B.C. and built a fortress on Kőhegy. Around 350 B.C., land-cultivating Celtic tribes arrived from the west, followed by the Eravisci of Celtic origin.

Although the continuity of the history of the ancient settlement often fades into the oblivion of the distant past, it seems certain that Szentendre reached its first golden age as a fortress of the province of Pannonia. In the 1st century A.D. the Romans incorporated Transdanubia into their empire and called this province Pannonia. Aquincum became the military and civilian centre of the eastern half of the province (Pannonia Inferior). Located between Aquincum and Cirpi (Dunabogdány), Ulcisia Castra—the predecessor of present-day Szentendre—became the northernmost point of the Danube Bend, a strategically important link in the *limes,* the Roman Empire's vast fortress system. The name Ulcisia Castra (Wolf's Castle) was probably derived from the name of the Eravisci's ancient settlement. The military camp *(castrum)* was built in the 2nd century on the south side of the Bükkös Stream, in the centre of present-day Szentendre. (The collection of Roman Stonework Finds stands here today, along the new Dunakanyar Boulevard, stretching over the area between Rómaisánc Street and Paprikabiró Street.) The high stone walls of the fortress were fortified at the corners and the sides with watchtowers and gate-houses. Behind it lay the *canabae,* the camp town of the burghers, which was populated by artisans, merchants and soldiers' relatives. Further away, the province's officials, well-to-do merchants and officers built their luxurious villas, which were furnished with hot-air heating, terrazzo flooring, and adorned with colourful murals. They buried their dead along the road leading out of the town and it was here that they layed the tombstones. The stone relics of the Romanized Eravisci are particularly beautiful and fascinating. The garrison often changed; in addition to the soldiers of the Roman legions a group of Syrian archers were also stationed here at the beginning of the 3rd century, while in the 4th century Dalmatian cavalry guarded the camp which was given the name of Castra Constantia under Constantine II.

In the wake of nomadic attacks coming from the other side of the Danube, and following the invasion of the Huns who came from the steppes of Southern Russia, the Roman legions left the camp at the beginning of the 5th century. During the 6th and 7th centuries the camp probably became the tribal centre of an Avar prince. Rich archaeological find dating from the early 7th century discovered in Szentendre (women's jewellery, Byzantine gold coins, weapons, saddlery) seem to substantiate this conjecture. After the fall of the Avar Empire the region was populated by Slavs, although no relics of their life have been found in or around Szentendre.

At the end of the 9th century the Magyars occupied the Carpathian Basin and settled in the region of the Danube Bend, putting an end to the turbulent centuries of the Great Migrations in this area. At the turn of the 9th and 10th centuries, this region belonged to the conquering princes Kurszán and Árpád. Under King Stephen I (1001–1038), Szentendre was part of Visegrád County and came into the possession of the Veszprém Bishopric. Although it had existed as a settlement as early as 1009, Szentendre is first mentioned by name in a document written in Latin and issued by King Géza II in 1146: *"Actum est… in curia episcopali S. Andree secus Danubium",* that is, written in the bishop's manor house in the Danube in Saint Andrew.

Szentendre probably received its name from the apostle St. Andrew, the patron saint of the town's medieval parish church, although the church on "Kliszsza", or "Church Hill" (nowadays called Castle Hill) which still stands today and has been rebuilt several times over the centuries, was built in the 12th century in honour of St. John the Baptist. Some hold the view that Szentendre was named after King Andrew, the son-in-law of Yaroslav, prince of Kiev. King Andrew I was baptized on Russian soil and founded a Greek Orthodox monastery in honour of the Apostle Andrew who, as legend has it, founded the Russian Eastern Church and was the patron saint of the Russians. The town was popularly known as Szentendre after 1358, though the name Szent-András continued to crop up occasionally up to the end of the 17th century. "Sentandreja" (or "Sentandrija"), the Serb variant of the name, comes from the Hungarian and surfaced after 1690.

Comparatively little is known of medieval Szentendre. The only important building to have survived, the one which probably towered over the centre of the medieval settlement, is the town's Romanesque church, which was destroyed in 1294 by the Johannite knights of Esztergom. The 14th and 15th-century details, which were added at a later date, are even more conspicuous today. The carved Gothic stone sun dial on the south-west buttress of the tower is a highly fascinating detail.

Up to 1333, the rural settlement, which soon grew into an agricultural town, was the seat of the deanery of the Veszprém Diocese. A papal bull issued in 1226 mentions it as an archdeaconry. It remained an ecclesiastical estate throughout the Middle Ages, though in 1318 it was, for a few years, incorporated into the royal estate which was added to Visegrád Castle. This, however, did not affect the town's development. By the 12th and 13th centuries Szentendre was almost certainly a major settlement. The descendants of the conquering Magyars cut down the forests, and began to till the land. Although Szentendre also suffered from the devastating Mongol invasion of 1241, it survived the catastrophe and its development continued uninterrupted.

The proximity of the royal seats—Esztergom, Visegrád and later Buda—boosted Szentendre's development; however, the town also had to share their fate, when Ottoman expansionism put an abrupt end to Szentendre's prosperity. After the occupation of Buda in 1541, Szentendre became part of the estate of the pasha of Buda and remained so for one hundred and fifty years. By the end of the 16th century it was almost completely deserted. According to Turkish records there were only between three and six households in Szentendre during the 17th century. In the course of the battles preceding the re-capturing of Buda in 1686, the medieval agricultural town was totally destroyed. Pursued by the victorious armies of Charles of Lotharingia, the last pasha of Buda pressed south, destroying everything in his path.

The 18th century marked the beginning of a new period of prosperity for Szentendre. Following Eugene of Savoy's unsuccessful Serbian campaign and the capitulation of Belgrade, large numbers of Serb insurrectionists led by Patriarch Arsenije Crnojević of Ipek (Peć) settled in Szentendre in the autumn of 1690. The Serbs sought refuge in Hungary to escape Ottoman reprisals. According to a contemporary account, about fifteen hundred Serb families, a total of 8,000 people, settled in Szentendre at the end of the 17th century. The name of Izbég still preserves the memory of the settlement of the Serbs in Szentendre (zbeg—'refuge'), while the memory of the Serb Patriarch Arsenije Crnojević has been preserved by the popular name Stara Voda, the Water of the Old Man.

The Serb settlers were soon followed in Szentendre by Hungarians, Germans, Slovaks, Greeks as well as Macedo-Rumanians from the Balkans and Catholic "Dalmatians". The bustling life of this small town, rapidly developing at the beginning of the 18th century, was enriched by this cavalcade of many nationalities, tongues, religions, customs and calendars. Almost overnight, Szentendre emerged as a comparatively large settlement with a growing population. The new Szentendre took shape around the medieval core of the town. The new settlers found only ruins here—the remnants of the medieval parish church that towered over "Klissza" Hill. There were probably a few delapidated houses in today's Görög Street, and the Serb settlers found the Roman fortress, which defied the devastating current of time and history, comparatively intact. Its fate, however, was sealed by the hectic building activity of the new settlers; its walls were demolished and the stones incorporated into new buildings. Nevertheless, initially timber was the most widely used building material. As early as 1690 the monks of the Serb Ravanica Monastery built a tiny church out of wooden beams on the bank of the Danube. Here they placed the relics of the Serb Czar Lazarus, which took forty days to carry to the church on foot. A monk who wrote the chronicle with this interesting bit of information also gave special mention to one other detail, namely that they had found a good harbour at the town's shore.

The outlines of Szentendre's captivating townscape began to emerge during the middle of the 18th century and, as far as the town's core itself is concerned, it has retained its original beauty almost intact. Szentendre's prosperity was closely linked with its lively trade. Credit for the latter must go to the craftsmen, who formed guilds, and to the vine cultivating farmers. Szentendre's Serb Merchant Society was granted its first franchise in 1698, but guilds were also formed by quilt and smock makers, bootmakers, tanners who made morocco and cordovan leather, furriers, tailors, soap boilers, shoemakers, blacksmiths, locksmiths and wheelwrights. Vine cultivation flourished in Szentendre after the settlement of the Serbs. Their red wine was especially famous and the "Serb Vermouth" and "aszú" wine was known even in distant countries. According to contemporary statistics, the quantity of wine made in Szentendre rose from 3,459 *urnas* in 1730 to 30,214 *urnas* in 1771 (1 *urna* = 62.5 litres). Under the reign of Joseph II, Mátyás Ráby recalled Szentendre as follows: "Its situation is extremely pleasant, it has several vine hills where splendid grapes are grown, its population surpassed six thousand souls. The Serbs living there conduct a lively commerce in wine with several European countries. Its situation and buildings surpass many distinguished towns in more than one respect." The carts and ships of Szentendre's merchants reached Austria, Bohemia, Poland, Russia and, to the south, even went as far as the Ottoman border fortress region.

To this day, Szentendre's townscape is dominated by seven towers. The medieval parish church, which in 1710 was reconstructed in the baroque style, stands on Castle Hill. In the town centre, on an area of just a few hundred square metres, six splendid 18th-century baroque churches, built by the Serbs, face east. Their names serve as reminders of the ancient homeland of their constructors, who had come to settle in Szentendre. (In 1766, Izbég was annexed to Szentendre, thereby enriching the town with yet another church.)

According to a contemporary account, the new inhabitants of the town built their low houses first on the bank of the Danube and along the flat area beside the river. Even in those days, there was a long row of shops and workshops at the market (today's Marx Square). During the early decades the town's shopping district was in many ways reminiscent of the East and the Balkans. Before long, the colourful and embellished façades of the houses of the well-to-do burghers, artisans, merchants, wine makers, patricians and noble families lined the streets surrounding the churches. The merchants' houses were built with *entresols*, used to store goods, and with attics, while under the houses of the wine producers stretched long cellars, the entrances to which opened directly from the street. The multi-storey houses of the wealthy burghers, nobility and patricians were concentrated in the heart of the town, while the single-storey rural houses of the farmers were mostly confined to the outskirsts. Baroque portals, well-proportioned, balconied rococo, Louis-Seize, neo-classical façades, ornamental wrought-iron railings and gates alternated. The townscape was fashioned by distinguished master builders from Pest-Buda and talented local builders. Architects from distant lands also came to Szentendre, among them Andreas Mayerhoffer, from Salzburg. It was on the basis of his plans that the Serb Blagoveštenska (Annunciation) Church, one of the town's most beautiful baroque monuments, was built in the main square. The pictures of the splendid, richly carved, monumental gilded iconostases are the work of Serb, Russian and Hungarian icon painters from Buda, Karlóca and Szentendre itself.

Imperial privileges ensured prosperity for the burghers of Szentendre. However, the memoirs of Mátyás Ráby indicate dismal feudal conditions. Mátyás Ráby was a man of tragic fate who, in 1784, was despatched by Joseph II to investigate the excessive abuses of power and tyranny. The story of his eventful life is told by the popular 19th-century Hungarian novelist Mór Jókai in *Rab Ráby,* while an authentic portrayal of the life of Szentendre's society was provided by Jakob Ignjatović, the founder of realist Serb prose, in the novel entitled *The Eternal Groom.*

At the end of the 18th century, Szentendre, an agricultural town, became a chartered royal town, which entailed further privileges. In spite of this, however, the town's economy gradually declined in the course of the 19th century. At the beginning of the 1880s, the perishing of the famous vineyards shook the rudiments of Szentendre's agriculture and marked the end of vine cultivation in the area. Even early industrial development brought no breakthrough in the town's economy. At the same time, the proximity of the sprawling capital city, Budapest, brought about the re-stratification of its population.

Today, Szentendre, which had a population of five thousand at the turn of the century, has seventeen thousand inhabitants. Moreover, during the summer months it has to accommodate another ten to twelve thousand vacationers as well. Szentendre is one of the most popular tourist spots of the Danube Bend. One and a half million tourists flock to this enchanting little town from every part of the country, from the neighbouring countries, and even from distant lands.

More recent additions to this historical town include a modern residential area and a new motorway which joins Szentendre to the capital city, Budapest. Its railway service links directly onto the Budapest Metro, while it can also be reached by boat.

Szentendre has always attracted painters. The finest masters of modern Hungarian painting have depicted its houses, streets, motifs and landscape. Many even chose to settle here. The town's many museums and galleries exhibit the outstanding works of contemporary Hungarian fine art. There are also museums dedicated to the Ferenczy family, the sculptor and ceramic artist Margit Kovács (1902–1977), which is the country's most frequented museum, to painters Béla Czóbel (1883–1976), János Kmetty (1889–1975) and the sculptor Jenő Kerényi (1908–1975). There is also a special collection of paintings by Jenő Barcsay, while the Szentendre Gallery stages temporary exhibitions of painters living in Szentendre.

The Collection of Serb Ecclesiastical Art presents

five centuries (15th–19th c.) of Church art, including icons of the Eastern Church.

Located around Liberty Spring, the Open-Air Village Museum (Skanzen) presents the traditional forms of Hungarian folk architecture. The exhibits have been brought to the museum from every part of the country and are displayed on a regional basis.

Szentendre is also the cultural centre of Pest County; the Pest County Cultural Centre and Library is the heart of the county's cultural life.

Every summer tourists flock to Szentendre to see the productions of the Szentendre Open-Air Theatre and other colourful and spectacular programmes. For example, to the delight of locals and visitors alike, the Dalmatian tradition of St. Ivan's Day fire-jumping is still very much alive in Szentendre, as is the spectacular Serb festival on the 19th August.

"...Magnificent landscape, prosperity, superb wines, heavenly water. Who could ask for anything more?"

Stojan Vujičić

1

1–3 During the 18th and 19th centuries, the Main Square was the centre of life in Szentendre. The square, which has preserved its historical character, has the shape of an irregular triangle.

   It is surrounded on all sides by late-baroque, rococo and neo-classical burghers' and merchants' houses. Numerous streets, mews and alleys run into the square in the centre of which stands the ornamental baroque memorial cross (1763) of the Serb "Privileged Merchant Society" (guild), also known as the Votive Cross. At the beginning of the 20th century, the town's whipping post also stood here. The square's one-time colourful cavalcade of artisans and merchants has been replaced by the cavalcade of tourists who visit Szentendre all the year round.

4

5

4 In addition to the characteristic stylistic traits of their period, the houses of Szentendre's merchants and artisans also bear other characteristic marks. The *entresol,* the ridged, high gabled roofs, the big baroque portals with curb stones, and the cellar entrances securely locked with wrought-iron wing-gates all bear witness to the occupations of the town's former inhabitants. Local legend links the large semi-detached house with a cellar entrance at Rab Ráby Square 1 to the figure of Jókai's famous hero, Mátyás Ráby, the protector of the poor, who led an eventful and adventurous life and suffered a tragic fate. The house was probably owned by a large and wealthy wine producing family. An anonymous sculptor carved a bunch of grapes on the keystone of its gate and the date 1768, the year the house was built, on every corner.

5 A coat of arms held by two lions can be seen on the façade of the former merchant's house situated on the corner of Dumtsa Jenő Street and Péter–Pál Street (18th century).

6 A typical Szentendre portal with cellar entrance closed off by wrought-iron door wings (Dumtsa Jenő Street 4).

7 Although to some extent it has followed the old core of the medieval settlement and has adjusted to the relief of the hillside descending upon the Szentendre branch of the Danube, Szentendre's townscape as we see it today at the turn of the 18th and 19th centuries. The narrow streets of the old settlement, which led from the Danube to the parish church erected on Castle Hill, such as today's Görög Street with its few stone houses, already existed at the time. Today's Main Square (Marx Square) also emerged on a flatter terraced section of the coastal hillside and was probably the junction of the old Szentendre. According to a contemporary account by a monk teacher from Ravanica called Stephen, the new Serb population who settled in Szentendre at the end of the 17th century, "settled above Buda, in a place called Szent András", where they found a good harbour. However, they found the settlement in ruins after the expulsion of the Turks from Hungary. For a few decades buildings were primarily built from timber and logs, for which the neighbouring woods supplied abundant building material. Reed was also available in abundance along the Danube, and houses could be built from adobe with walls made from plastered wickerwork. However, by the 1740s, a host of often ostentatious burghers' mansions and ornamental baroque churches sprung up in accordance with the latest architectural know-how. The number of baroque churches was glaringly out of proportion with the size of Szentendre's population. Up to the middle of the 19th century, Szentendre's wide-ranging trading activity, handicrafts industry and, above all, the prosperous wine producing sector provided the financial backing for enterprises of this nature. Standing in the town's Main Square is the Greek Orthodox Blagoveštenska (Annunciation) Church, Szentendre's most beautiful baroque monument. It is also called the "Greek" Church, perhaps because of the Greek epitaph in its wall facing Görög Street (1759), or perhaps because of the Greek language liturgies that were once held in it at the request of Szentendre's Greek families. It was first built from wood in 1690 and later, between 1752–1754, was transformed into the baroque church it is today, probably on the basis of plans by Andreas Mayerhoffer, the finest master of baroque architecture in Pest.

8 Main gate of the Blagoveštenska Church
9 The paintings of the ornately carved and gilded iconostasis are the work of Mihail Živković (1776–1824), a Serb painter who lived in Buda, and were made between 1802 and 1804.

10 Rococo wrought-iron window grilles on the building of the Margit Kovács Museum in Görög Street (18th century).
11 Corner balcony of an 18th-century Serb merchant house at the lower end of Görög Street, by the Danube, with the Blagoveštenska (Annunciation) or "Greek" Church in the background.

12 Townscape with spires from the Danube: the Catholic Parish Church, the Serb Orthodox Episcopal Cathedral ("Belgrade Church") and the Blagoveštenska (Annunciation) or "Greek" Church.

13 The Catholic Parish Church on Castle Hill,
the former Klissza (12th–18th c.).
14 The characteristic ridge (1924) of the main façade
of the Town Hall, which can also be seen in Szentendre's coat of arms.

14

15 Váralja Steps at Town Hall Square, with the tower of the Catholic church. A memorial plaque on the parapet wall reveals that in 1980 the Hungarian Town Planning Society awarded the János Hild medal to the town of Szentendre.

16 The labyrinth of its irregularly shaped squares, whimsically meandering cobble-stone streets, narrow alleys, winding ascents and stairways imparts a Mediterranean character to the town, evoking the atmosphere of Dalmatian, Greek and Italian coastal towns.

17–18 The famous roof-tops of Szentendre

19–20 The inhabitants of the growing settlement concentrated around Castle Hill and the bank of the Danube not only cultivated the land but also pursued commerce: their goods were transported by carts and Danube ships. Their grain mills were powered by the Danube current.

2

21 Tourists in Church Square with the tower of the Blagoveštenska (Annunciation) Church in the background
22 Toys for sale
23 Street concert in Rab Ráby Square
24 Folklore display
25 Stage of the Szentendre Open-Air Theatre in Marx Square

26–27 "Antiquities" and "Volkskunst" for the tourist
28 Tourists in Görög Street. One and a half million
tourists visit Szentendre every year.

26

27

29–30 The Nostalgia Coffee-house in a former Serb merchant's house (Vörös Hadsereg Street 2)

31 The steep cobblestone stairway of Ferenczy Károly Mews
32 A house in Szerb Street

33 Cobblestoned Alkotmány Street at Marx Square, with the entrance of the Nostalgia House and the Aranysárkány (Golden Dragon) Restaurant
34 Alkotmány Street 10/B: a gate below Castle Hill

35 The alley of Váralja Steps at Marx Square
36 Avakumović Mews with the Serb Orthodox Episcopal Cathedral (between Alkotmány and Hunyadi Street), carry a Mediterranean atmosphere.

37

38

37 Baroque epitaph on the wall of the Serb Orthodox Episcopal Cathedral, with the coat of arms of the Margaritović family (1778).
38 18th-century tombstone at the stone fence of the Serb Episcopal Cathedral.
39 The ornate gate of the Serb Orthodox Episcopal Cathedral on Alkotmány Street, with the coat of arms (1760s) of Buda's Serb Orthodox Diocese in its cartouche. Szentendre has been the second seat, alongside Buda, of Buda's Serb Orthodox bishops since 1690. The cathedral, which is traditionally called the "Belgrade Church", was constructed in 1763 where a smaller church built in the late 17th century had once stood. Rococo wrought-iron gates lead from Alkotmány and Hunyadi Street into the shady church garden, once the burial place of Szentendre's prominent Serb families. The gates were made by a local master locksmith, Márton Ginesser, in 1772.

40 Embossed silver cover of the Gospel from the 1730s (Collection of Serb Ecclesiastical Art)

41 Bishop's mitre made in Vienna, *c.* 1860 (Treasury of Buda's Serb Orthodox Bishopric)

42 Filigree hand crucifix with enamel insert depicting the Resurrection from the 19th century (Collection of Serb Ecclesiastical Art)

43 Archangels. Icon from the old iconostasis of Szentendre's Archangel Michael's (Požarevačka) Church, Szentendre, 1742 (Collection of Serb Ecclesiastical Art)

3

51–52 Wells in Rab Ráby Square. Szentendre's baroque wells have been a popular motive with painters ever since Károly Ferenczy's time. Today they are merely picturesque requisites of the townscape.
53 The cross of the tanners' guild and the tower of the Serb Preobraženska (The Lord's Transfiguration) Church (Bartók Béla Street 10) from the Szamárhegy.

54 Summer cottages on the slopes of the Pismány.

51

52

3

55 Jenő Kerényi Museum (Ady Endre Street 6). In the foreground: "Floating" (1959). The works of Jenő Kerényi (1908–1975) are characterized by dramatic expressiveness and powerful composition.
56 The statue of painter Béla Czóbel at the Artists' Colony (the work of Imre Varga)

57–59 The works of Margit Kovács (1902–1977) in Hungary's most frequented museum (Wastagh György Street 1). A sculptor and ceramic artist, Margit Kovács was one of the pioneers of Hungarian ceramics and was primarily attracted by folk art-inspired figural delineation.

60 Lajos Vajda (1908–1941): "Dappled Houses" (1936). Vajda's œuvre reveals a painter of European standing. In his surrealistic pictures Szentendre's baroque motifs —the spires/towers of the Orthodox churches, the symbols of the epitaphs and the often enigmatic Eastern Church icons—reflect his very personal view of the world.

61 The 18th-century frescoes on the vaulted ceiling of the Szentendre Gallery (formerly a Serb merchant's house) depicting Mark the Evangelist and Archangel Michael were uncovered when the building was restored.

62–63 János Kmetty "Winding Szentendre Street"
(1940). János Kmetty (1889–1975) was the consistent
cultivator of the Cézanne trend. He was a painter with
an affinity for Cubism who spent his summers working
in Szentendre. János Kmetty Museum (Marx Square 21).

65

64–65 Jenő Barcsay:"Szentendre houses" (1963). The Jenő Barcsay Collection is located in a house built in 1801 (Dumtsa Jenő Street 10). Jenő Barcsay (b. 1900) the leading master of contemporary Hungarian painting, has been working in Szentendre since 1924.

66–67 Béla Czóbel: "Girl with Fan" (1975). Béla Czóbel Museum (Templom Square 1). Béla Czóbel (1883–1976) began as a member of the Nagybánya School of *plein air* painting, studied in Munich and Paris, and lived in the Netherlands, Berlin, and from 1925 onwards, in Paris. During the final decades of his life, he lived alternately in Paris and Szentendre.

68

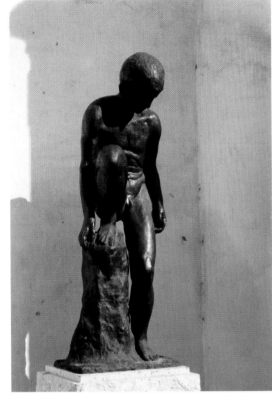

68–71 Painter Károly Ferenczy (1862–1917), a leading master of the Nagybánya School of *plein air* painting, lived and worked in Szentendre between 1889 and 1892. His twins, sculptor Béni Ferenczy (1890–1967) and gobelin artist Noémi Ferenczy (1890–1957), were born here. A late-baroque (1793) Serb school building houses the Museum of the Ferenczy family.

Béni Ferenczy: "Little Alpinist" (1953), in Alkotmány Street.
Károly Ferenczy: "Gardening Boy" (1891)
Noémi Ferenczy: "Budding Tree" (1946)

69

70

72–74 The Serb Orthodox Preobraženska (The Lord's Transfiguration) Church was built between 1741 and 1746 in place of an old wooden church. Its huge, ornate iconostasis, which stretches up to the triumphal arch, was painted in the middle of the 18th century by icon painters of Kiev. St. John the Baptist and the Virgin and Child from the iconostasis.

75–79 On 19th August every year a traditional Serb festival is held in the gardens of the Preobraženska Church which begins with a captivating pontifical ceremony. This is followed by the traditional grape consecration and a wild *kolo,* danced to the music of a tamboura orchestra. In the afternoon everyone is offered a drink of wine. The stalls of hucksters are part and parcel of the festival scene.

80 Designed by Imre Makovecz, the service centre in Marx Square is a fascinating attempt to incorporate modern architecture into Szentendre's historical environment.

81 The 18th-century Gallery House in Marx Square (seen from Török Mews) was a characteristic gable-roofed residential building with a verandah.

82–83 Cellar windows
84 House with balcony in Török Mews

85 The townscape with the Preobraženska Church and landing pier seen from the Danube

86–87 The late-baroque Louis Seize tower (1794) of
the Archangel Michael Serb Orthodox Church and
a detail of its iconostasis with the ornate "Czar's Gate"
(1742).

88 Stone carving at the collection of Roman
Stonework Finds (Rómaisánc Street) along the
Dunakanyar Boulevard
89 The Catholic Calvary from the second half of the
18th century (Kálvária Square)

90–93 The Open-Air Village Museum (Szabadság-
forrás út)

88

94 The Stara Voda (Old Spring, 1781)
95 The romantic branch of the Danube at Pap Island